How to Communicate Effectively With People

Tips for Building and Strengthening Your Speaking, Writing and Interpersonal Communications

How to Communicate Effectively With People

Tips for Building and Strengthening Your Speaking, Writing and Interpersonal Communications

by Deborah Shouse

SkillPath Publications

Editor: Bill Cowles

Cover design: Jason Sprenger

Layout: Barbara Hartzler

ISBN: 978-1-934589-05-2

Printed in the United States of America

Acknowledgements

Thanks to Sarah H. Shouse, M.A., Ph.D. Candidate for consulting on this book and for helping with the psychological context.

Thanks to my life partner Ron Zoglin for his careful reading, editing and excellent suggestions.

Thanks to Barbara Bartocci and Andrea Warren for their help with the editing process.

Thanks to the many wonderful writers and friends who are a constant source of inspiration and encouragement.

Table of Contents

Chapter 1:

Finding Your Charisma Quotient:
Be an ELECTRIC Communicator

Some people can stride into a group and instantly become the life of the gathering. Other people quietly press against the walls, eavesdropping on this conversation, throwing a crumb into that discussion, hoping to find the magic trail that leads to conversational success.

Moving from Mousy to Magnetic

Ellen had always thought of herself as a "wall-weed"—mousy, meek and forgettable. She rated her charisma quotient at sub-zero.

As you might imagine, for Ellen, the monthly after-hours Chamber of Commerce "meet and mingle" sessions that her company made her attend were pure agony. She was trapped for two hours in a room brimming with business professionals, each of whom seemed smarter, wittier, more attractive, more interesting and more dynamic than she was.

"They're just like you," her friend Samantha, a manic-mingler, assured her. "Only, they're in the middle of the room, stumbling into conversations, instead of against the wall, silent. Why don't you observe and listen and see what you learn?"

At the next mingling session, Ellen moved around a little, hovering on the edges of conversation and even standing in a conversation circle, listening and watching.

She learned some interesting things.

Observation opens conversation

"That's a fascinating tie you're wearing, Fred," one woman said. "What's the story behind that tie?"

Ellen had noticed the tie, too. It had Asian symbols woven into a forest green background.

Fred smiled and told the story of working in Tokyo for two years. His language tutor, whom he had studied with for six months, had given him the tie as a graduation present.

Fred's story brought up a lot of questions and a lot more stories.

With one observation, the woman had taken the talk from the weather to the world. She had involved everyone and made people feel like they were part of a fascinating conversation.

Curiosity creates conversation

Ellen rested against the wall and listened to two people talking about sports. She hated sports, or rather, she didn't know anything about them. As she listened, she realized one person was asking questions and the other was doing all of the talking.

Maybe the woman was like she was, not really knowledgeable about sports. But she seemed to know just enough to ask questions without seeming uninformed. Ellen noticed that the woman also seemed interested in the answers.

Experts are everywhere

One woman, a woman Ellen thought was dowdily dressed and seemed old and plain-looking, was doing a great job of circulating and connecting. Ellen moved closer to see what she was talking about.

"I'm curious," the woman said to a group of elegant-looking women, the kind of women Ellen was normally too shy to get close to. "I've been feeling so stressed lately, and I'd love to get your advice. What do you do when you're feeling stressed? How do you relax in the midst of chaos?"

Everyone had a tip and the woman listened intently, as if she were memorizing each idea. Ellen followed her around the room. This woman moved quietly into a group, listened politely to the conversation, and when it lagged, she asked her question. It seemed to work with both men and women and Ellen found herself listening carefully; the answers were interesting. The woman even turned to Ellen and asked her advice. Ellen surprised herself by having something to say.

She felt like an expert! Plus, she'd gleaned some good tips from everyone else.

At the end of the evening, Ellen felt relieved and confused. The people she saw making the best connections were not the smartest, most attractive or most well-dressed. They were just ordinary people, but they seemed to generate an **ELECTRIC** presence.

ELECTRIC means having:

- **E**nergy to pay attention and notice people
- **L**istening skills
- **E**nthusiasm for people's answers and conversations
- **C**onfidence that people want to talk to you
- **T**alking topics that draw people into the conversation
- **R**eaching-out abilities and a willingness to include everyone
- **I**nterest in observing your surroundings and asking questions based on what you see
- **C**onnections that are meaningful

Ellen decided she would work on "amping up" her own charismatic powers.

Plug Into Your Own Electricity

Think of a charismatic person you know and admire. What are some of their ELECTRIC qualities, like being dynamic and able to talk to anyone?

1. _____

2. _____

3. _____

4. _____

Now think of your own proclivities and abilities in a group. Choose the answer that most applies to you. If none of these captures you, write in your own answer.

1. My favorite kind of gathering is:

    A. A small group of good friends

    B. A large group, with tons of people I don't know

    C. A group with a few new people

    D. Other _____

2. I like a gathering where:

   A. I have a definite place to sit and people I like to sit with

   B. I have the freedom to move around and talk to whoever I want, whenever I want

   C. I have a place to sit if I wish, but I also can wander a little

   D. Other _____

3. When it comes to talking about things in groups:

   A. I can never think of anything interesting to say for myself

   B. I usually ask questions

   C. I like to discuss some issue that is going on in my life

   D. Other _____

4. A colleague says, "We're going to a large gathering. There's an hour of networking and mingling before the program." What is your response?

   A. Oh, my gosh. I feel a huge cold coming on.

   B. I can't wait to see who's there!

   C. Hopefully, I'll see someone I know. But I know I can do anything for one hour.

   D. Other _____

5. When I go into a group, I usually like to initially:

   A. Stand against the wall and observe things

   B. Make my way to the loudest, most vibrant group in the room

   C. Find one person to connect with

   D. Other _____

6. My goal when I go into a group is usually to:

   A. Live through it and get out as soon as possible

   B. Connect with as many people as possible

   C. Have one or two interesting conversations

   D. Other _____

Look at your answers.

- If you've chosen primarily A's, your charisma is more apparent when you're with trusted friends. It's time to explore ways to share your wit and wisdom with strangers.
- If you're full of B's, you're already comfortable with mingling. Now make sure you making the most of your connections, translating them into meaningful and valuable relationships.
- If you're choosing C's, you are great at one-on-one connections. You may want to learn ways to get more comfortable with a wider group of people.
- The D. Other answers give you opportunities to more deeply explore your own natural abilities.

Plugging Into Your Potential

Ellen wanted to learn to be more dynamic. She wanted to walk into a room with strangers and not feel her throat dry and her chest clutch. She wanted to feel comfortable speaking up in meetings. She yearned to be at the center of a lively conversation. She knew if she was more confident, more conversational and more visible, she would be more successful at work. And her personal life would also flourish. But she had no idea how to get started. She asked her friend Samantha for help.

"What are your goals?" Samantha asked.

"To walk into a meeting or party and know how to talk to people," Ellen said eagerly. "To feel like I have something to offer."

"You do have something to offer," Samantha said. "I can promise you that."

Samantha had asked Ellen to make a list of the things she liked about herself as a communicator.

Here are a few of the things Ellen, with some prompting from her friend, listed:

- An observant nature
- A naturally empathetic listening style
- The ability to ask good questions

Next Ellen made a list of areas she wanted to improve in. This time, she didn't need any help. She wrote:

- I feel I'm "not enough" in groups
- My voice gets squeaky when stressed
- My mind gets stuck: I can never think of anything interesting to say

What are your goals?

My conversational charisma goals:

1. _____

2. _____

3. _____

4. _____

What abilities do you already have? For example, are you able to tell a good story? Are you an excellent listener? Do you have an empathetic nature?

My natural abilities:

1. _____

2. _____

3. _____

4. _____

What areas do you want to improve?

My conversational challenges:

1. _____

2. _____

3. _____

4. _____

How will you benefit from improving your conversational charisma?

1. _____

2. _____

3. _____

4. _____

Who can help you build up your charisma?

Think of people who are comfortable in a variety of communication situations. You may want to choose someone who is a great networker, someone who can tell a compelling story and someone who's marvelous at facilitating a meeting.

Potential conversational coaches:

1. _____

2. _____

3. _____

4. _____

As you move through this book, use this list of abilities, challenges, supporters and benefits to help you meet your goals. You already have a lot of natural charisma—part of feeling confident and comfortable is appreciating your own gifts. Your supporters can help you understand and deepen the abilities you already have as well as improve the areas you find challenging.

Becoming the All-ELECTRIC Communicator

As you begin your journey to more effective communications, use the ELECTRIC acronym as a touchstone. Mastering these concepts will help you become the dynamic, confident, energized and well-respected communicator you want to be.

- Energy to pay attention and notice people
- Listening skills
- Enthusiasm for people's answers and conversations
- Confidence that people want to talk to you
- Talking topics that draw people into the conversation
- Reaching-out abilities and a willingness to include everyone
- Interest in observing your surroundings and asking questions based on what you see
- Connections that are meaningful

Chapter 2:

Impressing With First Impressions:

Make the Most
of Your I-CANS

You can probably make a list *of important firsts in your life: Your first day at school, the first person you loved, your first job, etc. One of the most important "firsts" is the first impression.*

First Impressions Are Not Fair

Sit in a busy area and watch the people walk by. Notice how quickly you form an impression of each person. Some, you instantly like. Some, you dislike.

If you were to talk to each of these people, your first feelings would be replaced by more authentic information. A person who looked angry might be a deeply compassionate person who was worrying about world hunger. A person who seemed cheerful and lively might have had two double espressos and be quite shallow and uninteresting to you.

Even though the first glance does not give you an accurate portrait of the real, complex person, people often judge others by those fleeting impressions.

Making the Most of the I-CANS

Ellen knew she could make a dynamite first impression if only she were:

- Smarter
- Taller
- Younger
- Better dressed

Everyone has his or her list of "if onlys." Talk to the most gorgeous woman you know and you'll find out she wishes she had straighter teeth, smoother skin or curlier hair. The most handsome man in the world probably thinks he needs to be taller, be more fit or have more hair.

Part of making a grand first impression is going beyond the "if onlys" and noticing what you do have and what you can add to an encounter.

First, make a list of all of the qualities that are most important to you. Do you value sincerity? confidence? resilience? friendliness? Then, pick the seven qualities that truly matter. Finally, circle your top three.

Best seven: Top three:

1. _____   1. _____

2. _____   2. _____

3 _____   3. _____

4. _____

5. _____

6. _____

7. _____

When you think about making a "good" first impression, think about how you can show some or all of those three qualities. The more you exhibit qualities that are important to you, the stronger the impression you will make.

No matter what your physical attributes or wardrobe limitations, make the most of your **I-CANS** and you'll create a stellar first impression.

- **Interesting**—Fortify yourself with interesting information. Listen for out-of-the-ordinary, uplifting or curious stories or facts. Such items can be the catalysts for great conversations.
- **Confident**—Even if you feel nervous, you can act confident. Do this by tuning into your seven most important qualities. You want to share and project those qualities. Before going to work, a meeting or a gathering, remind yourself—your goal is to show people who you really are. Stand up straight, relax your shoulders, adopt an easy stride and you will appear confident.
- **Attentive**—Paying a little bit of attention to a person goes a long way. Ask a question upon meeting someone and pay attention to the answer.
- **Notable**—Carry or wear something notable or unique, something that echoes who you are. If you are uncomfortable drawing attention to yourself, look for the notable things others are wearing or carrying. Use these notables to build on your first impression.
- **Smiling**—A smile speaks even when you can't figure out what to say. Project your feelings of warmth and your willingness to connect through your smile.

Review your **I-CANS** before you go into a new situation. Boost your first impressions by noticing which of the **I-CANS** come naturally to you and by analyzing situations when all of your **I-CANS** come through. The more you understand about your natural comfort level, the more you can expand that level to more challenging situations.

Set the Stage for Star-Quality First Impressions

Imagine you are a famous movie star or sports legend. Naturally, people are curious and are watching carefully to see what you are really like. They are analyzing your clothes, your facial expressions and your gestures. They are dissecting how you speak and to whom you speak. They are fascinated by what you are carrying around. These people are interested in your every move.

Even though most of us don't draw movie star attention, people do randomly notice us. Are you presenting yourself as the star you are? Do your ELECTRIC qualities shine through?

Here are some examples:

Ben, a financial planner, comes out to personally greet and escort each client instead of having his assistant send them in. He dresses professionally, adding a colorful tie for a splash of personality. He has a table ready so he can sit right next to the client, without a desk in the way. He has a copy of their portfolio at his fingertips. He wants clients to instantly think of him as smart, prepared and ready to serve them.

Miriam works as an administrative assistant for Ben and Joyce, also a financial planner. Joyce prefers to have Miriam escort her clients to her office. When clients come to the office, Miriam always personally welcomes them and offers them some refreshment. She makes sure they are comfortably seated and she contacts their advisor immediately. She wants the clients to think she is competent, attentive and alert to their needs.

Kate works as a home-health social worker. When she meets a new client, often a homebound elder, she wants the person to immediately trust her and feel comfortable talking to her. Kate walks into the home with a lively stride. She carries a briefcase and she wears comfortable and colorful clothes. She also wears a big smile and adorns herself with bright bracelets and sparkling rings. Even with vision problems, a client can hear and sense that Kate is someone he or she can feel at home with.

Creating Memorable Moments

Reaching out to others helps connect and create a good first impression

Ellen saw Kate at the after-hours networking meeting. She noticed her colorful clothes and ready smile. "Here is someone I might be able to talk to," Ellen thought.

Ellen walked over to Kate. As she drew closer, Ellen grew shy. She stood near Kate, but her mind went blank. She couldn't think of anything to say except, "What cheerful clothes."

Kate smiled. "Thanks. I work with homebound elders and I've learned that bright colors put them at ease."

Ellen asked a question about Kate's work. Kate asked about Ellen's work. Then she asked Ellen what she liked to do for fun. Usually people only asked about your job at these gatherings, but this felt different. Ellen felt that Kate wanted to know something about her beyond whether she had any networking connections.

"I like to go swimming," Ellen said.

Kate smiled and asked about her favorite swimming places. Before she knew it, Ellen was telling Kate all about the swimming hole on her grandparents' Mississippi farm.

When Ellen left the meeting, she thought about her interactions. She had a warm feeling about Kate. Kate had put her right at ease by offering her information, asking her a personal question, sharing a story and confessing that she often felt ill at ease at these gatherings. After talking to Kate, Ellen felt smart and interesting. She also found Kate easy to talk to. She felt like she could trust her.

After the gathering, Ellen realized she had done most of the talking with Kate. She had only asked Kate a few questions. She couldn't believe it. Kate knew a lot about her, but Ellen knew very little about Kate.

Kate had seen how shy Ellen was and how she lacked confidence. She also saw how sincere Ellen was and she appreciated Ellen's excellent listening skills. Kate felt a nice connection during the conversation and looked forward to talking to Ellen again.

Coaching for First-rate Impressions

Imagine you are one of Ellen's coaches. Think about her encounter with Kate and about her abilities and challenges from the previous chapter, and then see what you can add to this analysis.

1. How did Ellen make the most of her natural abilities during her encounter with Kate?
    Ellen has a naturally empathetic listening style. Her observant nature helped her notice Kate.

2. What got in her way?
    Ellen got stuck, feeling she was "not enough" and couldn't think of anything interesting to say. Even though the conversation went well, Ellen's feelings of inferiority prevented her from drawing Kate deeper into talk.

3. Did she use her I-CANS?
    Ellen used her Confidence to walk over to Kate. She paid Attention to Kate's questions. She Noticed Kate's glitter. She lost her Smile through nervousness.

4. What could Ellen do to make a stronger first impression?
    Ellen needs to keep her confidence strong. She needs to remember that she is as interesting as anyone else. She needs to not only listen, which she is great at, but also she needs to have the confidence to ask questions and invite the other person more fully into the conversation.

5. What other advice would you give Ellen?
    How about Kate? List the ways she used her I-CANS.

First Aid

Choose a day when you know you will be meeting new people. Try to be aware of the impressions you are making. Keep in mind your abilities and challenges and the qualities that are most important to you. Then use your own powers of observation and intuition to get closer to your goals.

First Impressions Self-analysis

Use this checklist to help you heighten your abilities and to feel more confident and comfortable meeting new people.

1. Describe the situation.

   What was the setting? _____

   What types of people were you meeting? (Colleagues, managers, vendors, etc.)

   _____

2. Describe your behavior. Check your I-CANS quotient.

   Interesting? _____

   Confident? _____

   Attentive? _____

   Notable? _____

   Smiling? _____

3. Which of your qualities were you able to embody?

   _____

   _____

   _____

4. How many people did you connect with? _____

5. What were you proud of? _____

6. What would you like to have done better? _____

7. What did you learn? _____

Making a Good First Impression Every Day

"What's wrong?" Samantha asked Ellen one morning as Ellen walked into the break room.

"Nothing. Nothing's wrong. Why do you ask?"

"You didn't say hello, you didn't smile and you're hunched over," Samantha reported.

Ellen stared at Samantha. She had thought she was keeping her feelings under wraps, but Samantha had seen right through her.

"I'm going to a cocktail party tonight in my new neighborhood," Ellen told her. "I'm petrified I won't make a good impression."

"Meanwhile, you probably didn't make a good impression when you came into the office this morning," Samantha said gently. "Did you even say hello to anyone?"

Ellen hung her head. "I didn't even think about that. I was too busy worrying about tonight."

Overturning troublesome impressions

Ellen felt terrible that she had ignored her co-workers and didn't say hello to them.

Samantha coached her on reversing any damage. "Simply tell them what was going on with you. Ask them for advice."

Ellen followed Samantha's advice. She had some great conversations and she also received extra tips about mingling. Plus, she learned many of her co-workers shared her fear of initial conversations.

Samantha's ideas helped Ellen repair the impression that she was too busy for others. Ellen was showing people that she was vulnerable and she was giving them attention and inviting them to be experts.

Every Day Is a First

Every day, you have a chance to build your charisma quotient and make a great first impression on the people you live and work with. They are the perfect audience to practice on, using the qualities that are most important to you and highlighting your natural abilities. This first connection can set the tone for that day's interactions.

When you treat people like the stars they are, they will usually treat you the same way.

Notice all the "firsts" in your day. These include:

- First greeting of the day
- Opening of a meeting
- First e-mail to someone that day
- First telephone contact
- Other firsts:

_____

_____

By paying attention to these everyday "firsts," you can easily improve and deepen connections throughout the day.

ELECTRIC First Impressions

In this chapter, you've gone beyond your "if-onlys" and moved into your I-CANS. You've seen how to use **these** ELECTRIC skills to light up first impressions:

- **Energy to pay attention and notice people**
- **Listening skills**
- Enthusiasm for people's answers and conversations
- **Confidence that people want to talk to you**
- Talking topics that draw people into the conversation
- **Reaching-out abilities and a willingness to include everyone**
- Interest in observing your surroundings and asking questions based on what you see
- Connections that are meaningful

What if you could walk into any gathering or situation with a feeling of excitement and esteem? You have something interesting to offer and you have the willingness to hear what others have to offer you. That knowledge makes every encounter and every event an adventure!

Chapter 3:

Mastering Mingling:

Connect Easily
With a Group

The Adventure Begins:
Creating Conversations That Connect

Miriam got to the conference center early, to help Joyce and the other financial planners set up for the client dinner and seminar. Despite her confidence around clients, Miriam often felt a little uneasy around the financial planners. She felt shy and unworthy. She wanted to project her competent, attentive and alert qualities so Joyce would be proud of her. But every time she attended one of these seminars, her self-doubts tried to take over.

Even though she had set up many conferences and had total confidence in her ability to manage the details, Miriam entered the conference center with her head bowed. She did not radiantly smile at everyone. She hurried to her station and got everything ready. She was so efficient that she was ready a full half hour before the guests were due to arrive.

One of the other financial planners, Ben, beckoned to her. "I'm setting up the brochures and handouts for my presentation," Ben told her. "Can you help me with this display?"

Miriam nodded. She easily created a visually pleasing display and organized Ben's handouts. As she finished Ben said, "You're quite efficient. How did you learn your organizational skills?"

Miriam stopped to think. Most often, she said, "I just picked them up," or "Anyone can do this," when someone complimented her. But she'd noticed those comments seemed to be conversation-stoppers.

Miriam said, "I was the oldest of six children and we had a very disorganized mother. So from early on, I was interested in the easiest ways to get organized. I started reading books on the subject in high school."

Ben nodded. "It's interesting how your background can influence your interest. Our family was always tight on money. Even as a kid, I was fascinated by how money works. I started an investment club in high school."

Miriam slipped into an easy and interesting conversation with Ben, asking questions about the investment club and telling him about the business she started when she was 14, organizing her neighbors' kitchens.

When Joyce came over, it was easy for Miriam to include her in the conversation, by recapping their discussion and asking Joyce how she got interested in financial planning.

By the time the first client arrived, Miriam was centered and ready to be part of creating a memorable evening.

Mingling Is Not for Sissies

Meaningful mingling takes flexibility, curiosity and openness.

We get into conversations for different reasons at different times and in different settings. Here are some of the reasons we enter into conversation:

- **Information**—to learn from the person we are talking to
- **Contacts**—to network or connect with the person on a business level
- **Friendship**—to get to know more about someone on a personal level; for some, this is the foundation for business networking
- **Convenience**—we need someone to talk to at a gathering

We've all left a conversation feeling buoyant and connected. And we've hurried away from a conversation feeling drained and irritated. A connective conversation is as good as GOLD:

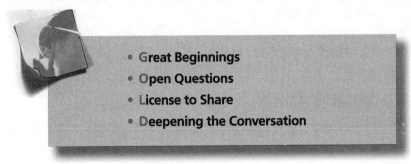

- **G**reat Beginnings
- **O**pen Questions
- **L**icense to Share
- **D**eepening the Conversation

Here are some of the GOLD components that made the interaction between Ben and Miriam connective and meaningful:

Great Beginnings

Ben started the conversation by noticing something positive about Miriam. That compliment helped introduce a warm tone.

Here's where your notables and noticing can come in handy. Be attentive and notice what people are wearing, carrying or doing. Then you can start your conversation with a compliment or observation and deepen the talk by seeking more information through a question.

Other Great Beginnings:

- Simply observe: "I see you're carrying *The Wall Street Journal*. What section of the paper do you find most valuable?"

- Invite expertise: "I've been overwhelmed by the demands of life recently. What do you do to regroup and slow down?"

- Exchange information: "The food here is terrific. I've had a lot of luck with good food recently. Just last week, I ate at Thai Orchid and it was marvelous. What are some of your favorite restaurants?"

If you can't think of anything to say, a warm smile and the simple question "How has your day been so far?" can work just fine.

Open Questions

Ben was seeking information. He asked an open-ended question that Miriam could not answer with a simple "yes" or "no."

Some tips for Open Questions:

- Choose a universal topic, something easy to answer. Try to steer away from topics that are divisive or depressing, such as politics or war. Try also to introduce topics that are fresh and exciting, something beyond sports and weather. Some examples of wide-open questions include: "What do you think …?" "Can you tell me more about …?"

- Ask a question that is general enough to lead to other questions
- When possible, ask a question that is interesting or surprising
- Open questions and universal topics make it easy to include a new person, even when the conversation gets personal

As you create your question, think about what you like to talk about. What do you have to offer to the conversation? What would you like to learn from or about this person? What would you like him to learn about you? Honor your time and energies and use your question to get started on a meaningful conversation.

License to Share

Miriam could answer Ben's question on either a business or personal level.

When inviting people you don't know well to share, give them options. Learn to craft questions that are wide enough so that people can:

- Share a personal story, if they wish
- Answer in a factual, impersonal way
- Answer succinctly, then move on to another topic

These kinds of questions keep the conversation comfortable.

Deepening the Conversation

Miriam decided to deepen the conversation and share some business-related and personal information. Her answer made it comfortable for Ben to continue sharing personal information. If Ben had felt uncomfortable talking about his interests as a boy, he easily could have returned to a business topic.

Sharing a story or revealing a personal vulnerability invites the conversation to move to a deeper level. The art is to be personal without making others uncomfortable. Here are some tips:

- Share information that most people can easily relate to
- Use humor whenever possible
- Show yourself as human and vulnerable, not as weak and wounded (That would be a much deeper conversation with a committed listener)

The Art of Inclusion: Out of the Ocean and Onto the Raft

Unfortunately, most of us know what it feels like to be left out of a conversation. We have experienced standing alone in a room full of talking, laughing people and feeling like we simply didn't belong or fit in. Most of us also have experienced the deep sense of gratitude and relief when someone reaches out and invites us into a conversation.

One simple way to be a memorable mingler is to master the art of inclusion. When you confidently enter the room, unless you need to talk to specific people, look for those who are standing alone and might truly appreciate being included.

When you are in a conversation and you see someone hovering outside your group, smile and invite them in. Introduce them. When possible, give them a business and personal "tagline" so people have a conversation starter. For example, you might say, "This is Joyce. She helps people make the most of their money. She's also a master gardener."

Give the newcomer an update on what you're discussing. For example, you might say, "We're just talking about our favorite restaurants." This allows them to move easily into the conversation.

When you reach out to invite in others, people will truly appreciate and remember your politeness, openness and generosity.

Saving Graces: Unsticking Gluey Conversations

Somehow, a fascinating conversation on the new downtown arts area deteriorated into a rant on the lack of federal funding. The wonderful interaction of the diverse group of five was silenced and one person held forth, repeating well-known bad news about lack of funding. Samantha liked this group of people and didn't want to move on yet, so she attempted something daring: a change of topic. She waited and waited … until the guy who was ranting took a breath. Then she said, "You know, talking about the arts makes me think of the time we went to the Smithsonian in Washington, D.C. Who else has traveled and been to art galleries?"

Several people smiled and eagerly latched onto the new topic. The monologuer eventually moved on to another group.

You may feel uncomfortable when you're trying to save a conversation. Do not be daunted if you have to try several times and take different tactics to change the topic. Some people possess an uncanny ability to hold forth even when those around them are itching for some talk time.

To unstick a glued-up conversation:

- Look for an entry point. This could be a pause for a breath or a word that offers you a transition.
- Don't worry about interrupting. Under these circumstances, you're doing a good deed.
- Give yourself permission to fail and try again.
- Start speaking confidently. Match the speaker's tone and enthusiasm.
- Pick a word or phrase and create a quick segue. It doesn't need to make perfect sense. For example, "And speaking of not having enough money, what do you think of …."

  Or, "You know, your comments on the government make me think of a fascinating article I read last week about the government of France. How many of you have traveled to that part of the world?"

  Or, using the same segue, you could ask a more open-ended question, "What kinds of trips have you all taken recently?"

Don't suffer needlessly at the words of a tyrannical talker. Save yourself and your group by interjecting another topic.

Bridge Conversations: From Dull to Dynamic

Ben was trapped in one of his least favorite conversations: health issues. He was sitting with a group of five financial planners. The others were taking turns, describing their latest health challenges. The discussion was getting more depressing by the moment. This was a brilliant group of men and women and Ben had looked forward to serious conversation with them. He watched for a natural lull and said, "Speaking of health, what do you think of the market this week?"

He planned to move from that general information to more gritty topics such as, "What techniques are you using to effectively work with clients in this down market?"

Creating a bridge from dull to dynamic is not easy. As with unsticking a conversation, you have to balance your desire to be polite with your desire to change the subject. Ben did not want to seem abrupt and possibly pushy. So he:

- Listened for a natural lull
- Spoke in a firm, confident voice
- Asked an open-ended question related to the previous topic
- Watched for an opportunity to move the conversation closer to his desired topic

Be a Boat, Not a Barnacle

The client conference went beautifully. The dinner was delicious. The presenters shared important financial information in an easy-to-digest manner. Miriam was saying good-bye to various clients when she got trapped in an uncomfortable conversation by a good client of Joyce's. Unfortunately, he seemed bent on telling her the grueling details of his recent religious conversion right when she should be mingling and saying good-bye. Normally, Miriam welcomed a spiritual conversation. But tonight, the timing was all wrong. She tried to come up with a polite way to extricate herself but nothing seemed to work. Finally, she said, "I see how important this experience was for you and I want to hear all about it. But right now, I have other responsibilities and I can't give you the full attention you deserve. May we continue another time?"

He looked at her for a long moment and Miriam clenched her hands, hoping she had not offended him. Then he said, "Well, yes, of course. It's getting late after all. Another time." His voice had a warmth that told her all was well. She then moved on to other people.

There are many reasons to move onto another conversation and there are many ways to politely do so. Here are some reasons for wanting or needing to move on:

- Like Miriam, you have other responsibilities
- You're at a loss for words; you don't know what to talk about next
- The conversation has moved into topics that don't interest you
- You're eager to meet and connect with other people
- You need to take a break and attend to other things or refresh your listening skills

To move on, thank the person for the conversation. If possible, mention one thing you really enjoyed about the experience. Tell the person you look forward to your next connection, if that is true.

If you have to interrupt a long monologue, break in as gently as possible. Acknowledge what they've been saying and explain why you need to move along.

If you're leaving a group that is in full swing, catch the attention of the person you're most connected to in the group, and let them know, through pantomime or gesture, that you enjoyed the discussion and you have to leave.

It's easy to barnacle onto conversation, hanging on like it's the only one you might ever have. Be a boat and trust that you'll sail into even deeper and more abundant waters. When the conversation becomes strained or boring, move on and try to connect with someone else.

Building Your Reputation Through Conversation Builders

When you are part of a wonderful conversation, you are building your reputation as an interesting person. When you help facilitate a fascinating conversation, you build your reputation as a compassionate leader. The more you are aware of the group dynamics, the more successful and caring you can be.

Choose a busy day that's filled with conversations. At the end of the day, ask yourself:

- What were the most memorable conversations?
- What made them interesting?
- What kinds of topics were we discussing?
- How did I participate and contribute? What worked really well for me in that conversation?
- What do I wish I had done differently? What got in my way of taking that action?
- What kind of help or encouragement do I need to improve my conversational skills?

By looking at your day in this way, you'll get a deeper understanding of what is important to you. You'll see where you're shining and where you're not. You'll discover more ways to be your authentic self as you improve and create your mingling magic.

Places to Practice Marvelous Mingling

Think about three places you can practice your everyday mingling. For example, at a meeting, in the break room or at lunch:

1. _____

2. _____

3. _____

List three groups of people that you'd like to have a better connection with:

1. _____

2. _____

3. _____

List three things you can do to create the deeper connection:

1. _____

2. _____

3. _____

List three people, perhaps people related to those groups, who can support and help you:

1. _____

2. _____

3. _____

Powering Up Your Mingling

In this chapter, you've explored ways to create fascinating and connective conversations. You've learned the GOLD components of good interaction and you've seen how to move out of conversations that are stuck or sticky. You've improved your powers of patter by heightening your abilities in the following highlighted areas:

- **Energy to pay attention and notice people**
- **Listening skills**
- Enthusiasm for people's answers and conversations
- Confidence that people want to talk to you
- Talking topics that draw people into the conversation
- **Reaching-out abilities and a willingness to include everyone**
- **Interest in observing your surroundings and asking questions based on what you see**
- **Connections that are meaningful**

Chapter 4:

Giving Attention and Getting Connected:

Create Rapport
and Build Trust

George was the life of any gathering. *He was witty and full of great stories. He always had a smile and a warm handshake. He treated Ellen kindly, remembering her name and asking how she was. If he was in the middle of a group, which he usually was, he welcomed her in. Ellen admired his amazing social skills. But when she thought about people she trusted, George did not show up on the list.*

"Do you like George?" she asked Samantha one day when they were having lunch together.

"He's a lot of fun," Samantha answered.

"Do you trust him?"

Samantha paused over her soup. "I have no reason to distrust him, but now that I think about it, I don't exactly trust him."

"Me neither. I wonder why?"

People can have some of the qualities of good communicators and still not have the skills to take the conversation or the relationship to a deeper level.

Take George, the "look at me" communicator. George was gifted at holding court and entertaining people, but he was not good at making personal connections. His stories were amusing anecdotes and great icebreakers. But once the ice had turned to water, George paddled away. He never shared personal information. He never hinted at a vulnerability. He never tried to get to know people. The only question he'd ever asked Ellen was, "Hey, how are ya?" And he kept on moving while she answered. George had conversational charisma but he didn't have connecting power.

Carol was a different story. Ellen had met her two years ago when Carol came to work at the company. Ellen had said a "Hello, pleased to meet you," and Carol instantly began sharing the details of the terrible work environment she had just left. In ten minutes, Carol had poured her tragic work history all over Ellen. Samantha rolled her eyes when Ellen asked what she thought of Carol.

"Stay away unless you want to be trapped for thirty minutes, listening to a long sob story," Samantha said.

Carol, the "woe-is-me" talker, was another kind of communicator who didn't build rapport or trust. Carol was friendly, outgoing and willing to share anything. But she wasn't appropriate in how, when and where she shared. She wasn't communicating to deepen trust; she was talking to dump her troubles. Carol didn't have the listening skills to connect with the listener.

Stacey was a great listener. She asked many questions. Sometimes too many. When Stacey was talking to her, Ellen felt like she was being grilled for an investigative television show. Stacey had an astonishing memory, remembering everything about everybody, including the names of children and spouses. But Ellen was also astonished at how little Stacey actually contributed to a conversation. When Ellen asked Stacey a question, Stacey artfully turned the focus back to Ellen.

"Do you think she has something to hide?" Ellen asked Samantha.

Stacey was the "Don't ask me anything" kind of communicator. She definitely listened, digesting the information and asking more questions. But she was merely an objective observer, not a conversational partner. She took in information, but she was not willing to make the connection through sharing her own stories.

Think about the people you know that you don't particularly trust. What qualities keep you from trusting them? For example: The One-Time Communicator treats you warmly one day, sharing stories and listening intently, and ignores you another time.

1. _____

2. _____

3. _____

Building Rapport Through Truthful Talking

Creating a feeling of trust and rapport takes a delicate balance of truthful talking and genuine listening.

Truthful talking includes:

1. Consistently communicating with courtesy and friendliness.

   Weeks ago, Kate went to an area-wide home health meeting and met Sally, head of a neighboring agency. The two had a meaningful conversation. Kate had since talked to Sally at a lunch-and-learn gathering. So when she saw Sally across the room at a seminar, she hurried over to connect with her friend. But Sally glanced at Kate, said a quick hello and moved on to talk to someone else. Kate stood still, trying to figure out what had just happened. Sally had used her name, so she had not forgotten her. Kate felt hurt and confused.

   Think about how you feel when someone gives you a genuinely warm greeting. Then think about your response when the same person ignores you two days later. Unfortunately, most of us have experienced inconsistency in people's behavior toward us. That sort of unreliability destroys rapport and trust.

2. Sharing stories and information that reveal something about your genuine self.

   While Kate was trying to figure out Sally's behavior, Angela, one of the nurses in her program, came up to talk to her. Kate glanced at her watch; Angela's stories sometimes were more a trap than a treat, and Kate felt like she never knew any more than before about Angela after listening.

   Anyone can tell a story or an anecdote. But not that many people can tell a story that captures the art of truthful talking and helps build trust and rapport. To create a trust-building experience, you want the story to be:

   - A natural part of your conversation
   - Appropriate to the occasion
   - Short and clear enough to be meaningful
   - Free of ego and of "sell"
   - Universal enough to inspire a similar sharing from the listener

3. Pausing on purpose.

Ten minutes went by. Kate listened carefully, waiting for Angela to pause so she could throw in her 13 magic words: "I'd like to hear more later, but I really need to go now."

She waited and waited, and finally interrupted Angela to excuse herself. She felt bad about her "rude" behavior, but she didn't know what else to do.

We've all been backed into a conversational corner by a non-stop talker. A vital part of truthful talking is speaking in respectfully small bites and then pausing. That pause invites the other person to elegantly enter the conversation without having to bulldoze in.

Building trust and rapport with genuine listening

Samantha had just returned from a conference on creating a more environmentally friendly workplace. Her co-worker Brian knew she'd been excited about the conference. But Samantha didn't know Brian well, so she was surprised when he asked about the conference and actually hung around to listen. He not only listened, keeping great eye contact, but he asked questions. He seemed like he really wanted to understand the concepts. Sharing the details helped Samantha reinforce what she had learned and reminded her she wanted to share this information with a lot of people.

You know how affirming it is when someone truly listens to everything you are saying. Genuine listening goes beyond asking questions and hearing answers. Genuine listening means you are able to FOCUS:

- **F**ocus on the person telling the story, rather than gazing around the room or answering your cell phone
- **O**ffer feedback and reflection by commenting on the portions that most impacted you
- **C**larify by asking questions as needed
- **U**se expressions and gestures to reflect your feelings
- **S**hare a similar story or situation to deepen the conversation

Try to remember: Turning genuine listening into acknowledging action

"Hey Cassandra, I went to that Web site you were telling us about last week," Ron said. "You were right; it was extraordinary. I'm integrating some of the pointers into our brainstorming meeting next week."

Cassandra looked at Ron in disbelief and then smiled. She often shared information with people, but she rarely received any feedback. She felt honored and acknowledged that Ron had actually listened to what she said and had taken action. She was eager to share more sites and to learn about some of Ron's resources.

Acknowledging past conversations and following through on recommendations are powerful ways to build rapport and trust. By trying the Web site, Ron was saying to Cassandra:

- I genuinely listened to you
- I was interested in your recommendations
- I trusted what you said and I wanted to know more

Even if you listen and don't take action, you still can honor and acknowledge the person and your previous conversations by rapport-building phrases such as these:

- "I thought about you yesterday during our planning session. I remembered what you said about setting short-term goals and…"
- "I found that trade magazine you mentioned. It was excellent."
- "How was the telephone conference with the California team? It was yesterday, wasn't it?"

The more you are able to genuinely acknowledge and follow through on previous conversations, the more people will feel a sense of comfort and rapport with you.

A Quick "Am I Listening?" Quiz

To hone your FOCUS skills, take this quiz after a conversation.

Ask yourself:

- Did I pay attention to what they said?
- Did I maintain eye contact and offer my full attention?
- Did I offer reflection or feedback, showing that their words impacted me?
- Did I ask any clarifying questions?
- Was I a partner in the conversation, sharing my own wisdom or story on the subject?

Who Do You Feel Rapport With?

Think about the people you trust. Make a short list of the qualities that make them trustworthy. For example, they may be reliable or able to keep a confidence:

1. _____
2. _____
3. _____
4. _____

The more you know about the qualities that engender trust, the more easily you can strengthen the communication skills that will help people feel comfortable with you.

List a few things you do that inspire rapport and build trust. For example, are you a careful listener? Do you always greet people warmly?

1. _____
2. _____
3. _____
4. _____

Are there any qualities you could strengthen to help you gain ever greater rapport and trust with others?

1. _____

2. _____

3. _____

List three people in your work life you'd like to have a deeper relationship with. Write down two things you could easily do to begin building rapport with each person.

1. Name: _____

   Action: _____

   Action: _____

2. Name: _____

   Action: _____

   Action: _____

3. Name: _____

   Action: _____

   Action: _____

The ELECTRIC Art of Rapport-building

Just the simple acts of Truthful Talking and Genuine Listening help you build trust and rapport and deepen your communications and connections. In this chapter, you've learned how to enhance your abilities in the following highlighted areas:

- Energy to pay attention and notice people
- **Listening skills**
- **Enthusiasm for people's answers and conversations**
- **Confidence that people want to talk to you**
- Talking topics that draw people into the conversation
- Reaching-out abilities and a willingness to include everyone
- Interest in observing your surroundings and asking questions based on what you see
- Connections that are meaningful

Chapter 5:

Listening Creatively:
Build
Relationships

We all know the delicious energy of feeling alive and connected to other people. *It's wonderful to feel like we have heard and we have been heard. Generating or encouraging these connective feelings helps you strengthen and build relationships.*

"How was your day?" Samantha's husband asked her, as they sat down to dinner.

Samantha thought about the complexities of her day. She'd designed a newsletter, talked to clients, attended a meeting and solved a design problem for another department. But the highlight of the day was the story she'd heard at lunch.

"I met someone new, someone who might turn into a friend," she told her husband. "Cassandra's a designer in another department and a bunch of us were at lunch today. She told me a fascinating story."

She told her husband the story. As a child, Cassandra loved to draw but her family didn't want to waste money on art supplies. So Cassandra starting drawing on anything she could find. It drove her parents crazy. She was into cartooning and one day she penciled a whole cartoon series on a roll of toilet paper, then re-rolled the paper and placed it in the bathroom. Her mother had a friend over and the woman went to use the bathroom before dinner. She returned to the dining room smiling. "I have never seen such an artistic toilet paper roll. Whoever did those cartoons is very talented."

"Please forgive my daughter," Cassandra's mother had said, giving Cassandra a hard look. "She gets carried away."

"I'd be carried away too if I had that much talent. You have great talent, my dear," she had said to ten-year-old Cassandra.

"That woman was the first person who saw me for who I hoped I was," Cassandra said. "That woman also changed the way my family treated me. I was lucky. So many artists never have anyone to encourage them. That's why we need to encourage and appreciate each other."

Samantha smiled as she retold the story. "Then we all talked about ways we liked to be encouraged and ways we could encourage each other," Samantha said. "I felt like I knew Cassandra at the end of that lunch and I also felt closer to the others."

You can help create a comfortable connection by offering **SOFAS:**

- **S**hare a personal story or anecdote
- **O**ffer meaningful information
- **F**ind common ground
- **A**sk questions and cultivate your common ground
- **S**end or offer invitations

SOFAS offer you easy ways to use your communication skills to build visibility and relationships.

Share Personal Stories: Once Upon a Time

Sharing a well-crafted and meaningful personal story is a great way to capture people's interest and imagination.

Think about some of the stories you've heard in the last week or so. Which of them stay in your mind? Which did you repeat to another person? List two stories that were interesting to you and write a few words about why.

1. Story (a brief sentence that sums up the story): _____

   _____

   Who told it? _____

   Why it was meaningful for me? _____

   _____

2. Story (a brief sentence that sums up the story): _____

   _____

   Who told it? _____

   Why it was meaningful for me? _____

   _____

Meet your inner storyteller

Samantha was excited about sharpening her storytelling skills. Ellen was intimidated by the idea of sharing personal stories.

"I always get tongue-tied," she told Samantha. "I always feel as though no one really wants to listen."

"I used to feel like that," Samantha said. "Then I started practicing my stories on safe people, so I had a chance to try them out and make them better before I told them in a more judgmental crowd. Before I told a story, I asked people, 'Do you have time to listen to a short anecdote?' That way, they committed themselves to listening. If someone's in a hurry, I'd rather hear it up front than figure it out from their behavior during my story."

Ellen had a day-long marketing seminar coming up. She would be meeting marketing managers from all over the country. This would be an ideal time to use all her skills and try to create some friendships.

First, Samantha told her to write down her storytelling fears. Ellen's list included:

- Looking stupid
- Forgetting what I'm talking about
- Being boring
- Having people stop listening before I'm done

What comes up for you when you think about telling a personal story?

List your concerns:

1. _____

2. _____

3. _____

4. _____

List your excitements!

1. _____

2. _____

3. _____

4. _____

Take your stories to work and build your career

Take this simple quiz and notice the ways you are already using stories. Circle the answer or answers that suit you the best.

1. What kinds of stories do you like to tell?
- Personal stories
- Stories about other people
- Stories about famous people
- Other

2. How often do you tell stories on a typical workday?
- Once
- Twice
- Three times
- Other

3. What kinds of people do you tell stories to?
- Co-workers
- Friends
- Family
- Others

4. What inspires you to share a story?
- Another story
- A lull in the conversation
- The desire to connect
- Other

5. What keeps you from a sharing a story?
- Shyness
- Not knowing people well enough
- Not wanting to draw attention to myself
- Not having any stories
- Other

When Ellen answered question 5, she circled every answer. Yet she really did want to be noticed and remembered.

Turn ordinary life into extraordinary stories

Ideally, when you share a personal story you are offering people ideas, inspiration and entertainment and you are building relationships in the process.

A story often answers the question: What will the hero do to get what she wants?

A story starts with a simple outline:
- There's something you want
- Someone or something is in the way of you getting what you want
- Despite the resistance, you figure out how to solve the problem and get what you want
- In the process, you learn something meaningful

To make the story memorable, you can add:
- An attention-getting beginning
- Humor and opportunities for you to laugh at yourself
- Emotion

- Dialogue
- Other memorable characters
- Concrete, visual language that helps people "see" what you're talking about
- A meaningful ending that brings out the universality of the story

A good conversational story is short, taking place in three to five minutes. (Of course, there are exceptions.)

When you're creating stories to help you build friendships and relationships, the storyteller:
- Puts himself/herself into the story
- Shares personal vulnerability
- Is able to laugh at him/herself
- Understands the audience and knows when to share a story
- Uses his/her natural gifts to add flair to the story
- Doesn't fret at mumbles and stumbles

Thicken the plot

Cassandra's story is a great example of a short personal story that builds relationships. Here's the analysis:
- She had something she wanted: She wanted to draw
- Someone or something was in the way of her getting what she wanted: Her family didn't want to give her the necessary supplies
- Despite the resistance, she solved the problem: She drew on toilet paper
- In the process, she learned something meaningful: Cassandra learned to follow her passion. She also learned the power of affirmation and encouragement. She realized many artists have no encouragement, so they should learn to encourage and help each other.

Cassandra's story was also a great way to jump-start sharing stories, additional information or a spirited conversation.

Offer Meaningful Information:
Be the Go-to Person

Cassandra was always looking at markets for freelance art. Occasionally, she found markets looking for freelance writing. She believed that collaboration got you further than competition. So she generously shared marketing information with those who were trying to sell their art and writing.

"Feel free to spread the word," she wrote on her marketing e-mails. People did. That meant artists, writers, managers and vendors who wanted to do art and writing often reached out to Cassandra to get on her marketing list.

As more people were her on e-mail list, Cassandra realized this was a great way to get connected with new people, build relationships and stay connected with friends. She often included an inspiring quote or a short personal anecdote, always something that included humor and a personal lesson she had learned.

Occasionally, people wrote back to her, excited that their work had been accepted into a magazine, on-line journal or newspaper. Cassandra then asked permission to share that news with the mailing list. With this simple monthly communication, Cassandra was building relationships.

How to become a go-to person

Offering meaningful information should be fun for you as well as helpful for others. To become a mini-expert, simply make a quick list of the kinds of information you like to collect.

- What kinds of information are you already learning or collecting that might interest others?
- Who would enjoy receiving this information?
- What is the easiest way to share the information?
- What are the benefits of sharing this information with these people?

You want to find the perfect match—information you enjoy that you can share with people you enjoy and want to know better.

Find Common Ground: Conversational Catalysts

Finding common ground is a great way to speed up the relationship-building process.

Make a list of the things you enjoy talking about. Include as many "universal" subjects such as pets, shopping, eating out, family, cooking, exercising, etc. as possible.

My preferred topics:

1. _____

2. _____

3. _____

4. _____

5. _____

Save more intimate subjects, such as spirituality and politics, for people you know well.

Now, think about the people you'd like to create a deeper relationship with. What kinds of topics do they like to talk about? (Write down several topics for each name.)

Name: _____

Topics: 1. _____

2. _____

3. _____

4. _____

Name: _____

Topics: 1. _____

2. _____

3. _____

4. _____

Notice what your common ground is. When you're with these people, practice focusing more on your common ground. Areas of common interest can be a starting point for sharing more personal stories and information.

Ask Questions: Cultivating Your Common Ground

Think of open-ended conversation catalysts you can use to explore your common ground. These are comments or questions you can use one-on-one or in a group to try to create more depth and connections.

Here are some examples:

If you are with people who love to work out or exercise, you can move from the gym to relationship-building by asking:

- What inspired your interest in fitness?
- How do the qualities you use in exercising translate into your business life?
- What do you do when you get tired of exercising and want to quit?

If you are a dog lover and you want to move from your adorable, amazing dog to something different, try:

- Tell you me about your pets growing up.
- What inspired you to get this dog?
- What have you learned from your dog?

If you are a gardener and want to "dig" deeper, try:

- What inspired you to start gardening?
- How did you learn about gardening?
- How have you benefited from working in the garden?

Send or Offer Invitations: A Host of Reasons

Even if you don't want to go to a party, it's fun to be invited. Sending people invitations is a great way to let them know you're interested in continuing the conversation. Make these invites low-key and agenda-free.

For example:

- Cassandra e-mailed 10 people and invited them to lunch with her on Thursday. She selected a cafeteria-style restaurant, with plenty of room and moveable tables and chairs. She didn't even ask for an RSVP. She just said, "I'd love to see you, if the timing is right. Just show up if you can make it." She made sure one of her friends could join her, so she wouldn't be eating alone.

- Ben learned of a sports show one of his clients was hosting after work. The event was free and featured free wine and appetizers and putting tips from a golf pro. His client told Ben, "Spread the word. We want a big crowd." This was a stress-free chance for Ben to invite his clients who liked golf and sports and also those potential clients he wanted get to know better. Some he called and some he e-mailed.

- Val worked for a large retailer. Twice a year they had a special sale and they let their employees invite 20 people each to come early and save more. Val's friends and acquaintances liked receiving her first-come-first-serve super-saver e-mails.

Inviting several people is a great way to reach out and let people know you're thinking of them. Inviting one person is a more direct way to connect and have time to really get to know each other. After her group lunch, Cassandra often reached out to one person she felt a special camaraderie with and invited her to lunch.

Your invitation to building friendships

For people you are trying to build friendships with, the invitation idea is:

- Free
- Low-key
- Quick; doesn't take too much time
- Factored into the workday or right afterwards
- Casual

Think of ways you could reach out with invitations:

1. _____
2. _____
3. _____

Think of the people you want deeper connections with:

1. _____
2. _____
3. _____

List two ways in the next several months you'd like to reach out to them:

1. _____
2. _____

Putting Your Name in ELECTRIC Lights

Turning your natural gifts into memorable communications is an easy and effective way to build and deepen relationships. In this chapter, you've explored using the below highlighted skills:

- **Energy to pay attention and notice people**
- **Listening skills**
- Enthusiasm for people's answers and conversations
- Confidence that people want to talk to you
- **Talking topics that draw people into the conversation**
- Reaching-out abilities and a willingness to include everyone
- Interest in observing your surroundings and asking questions based on what you see
- Connections that are meaningful

Chapter 6:

Revving Up Your Communications:

Use Your
Inner Power

The more stress people are under, the more widely their behavior can vary. We don't have control over how others speak to us, listen, react to us or express themselves, but we can use and hone our powerful communication skills so we can understand and "manage" or connect with them.

"Why can't people be better listeners?" Ellen wondered. She had finally worked up the nerve to share a personal story with a group and one of the people was looking around the room. Ellen wanted to jump up and down to get her attention. She didn't know whether to stop the story and ask the woman if everything was all right, or just bluster through. She tried to concentrate on what she was saying. But she kept thinking about that woman. Did she hate the story? Was she bored? Was she rude or was she just clueless? Finally, Ellen remembered what Samantha had told her: "Tell your story for the audience that is listening. Don't worry about those who aren't." Ellen stumbled a little, but she managed to end the story. The two people who actually were listening to her smiled and reflected on the meaning of the story. Ellen left the group feeling happy—and a little confused.

The power of a pause

Miriam called the client personally, telling him that Joyce was running late and needed to reschedule.

"That is the third time this month this has happened," he said angrily.

Miriam knew that was not the case. This was the first time Joyce had rescheduled. The client himself had broken appointments twice, once by simply not showing up, the other by calling an hour before the appointment. She wanted to defend Joyce and set the record straight. But she paused, not knowing what to say. That gave her time to simply listen to what was underneath the words.

"You sound upset," she said.

"Darn right I'm upset," he answered.

"Is there anything we can do to make the new appointment easier for you?"

"Schedule it on a Tuesday when my son can drive me and I don't have to worry about lining up transportation."

Miriam found a spot on the next Tuesday. "Would you like a reminder call on Monday?" she asked, wondering now if he had forgotten one of the meetings.

"Yes, that would be nice."

Miriam heard the softening in his voice and felt a sense of compassion as they ended the call.

Expanding the Power Grids

Of course, many of us feel the world would be a better place if more people would just listen. But most of us don't have the power to make people pay attention to us. We have to rely on understanding and using the internal personal power we do have.

Our inner power reflects our values and our authentic self, qualities that are uniquely ours. Harnessing and understanding inner power helps us fine-tune communications skills, so we can influence people and create connections.

Here are some of the things we can have **CLEAR** control over:

- **C**oping skills and flexibility
- **L**istening abilities
- **E**motional releasing
- **A**ttitude
- **R**esponses to others

Coping Skills and Flexibility

Some foods need a few extra ingredients and a little marinating before they are at their best. Coping skills are a kind of communications marinade.

If you have patience, a willingness to listen and think before you take action, and qualities such as openness and tolerance, you have the ingredients for outstanding coping skills and flexibility.

To liven up your coping skills, first notice the kinds of triggers, people and situations that tend to irritate or incite your emotions.

For example, Ben is triggered by people who talk too much. Miriam feels challenged when she's around people who stand too close to her. Ellen finds it difficult to be in a situation where she might be put on the spot and asked to state her opinion.

Make a short list of your own challenges:

1. Trigger topics (your hot buttons): _____

2. Challenging types of people: _____

3. Difficult situations:_____

If you know that you're going to face one of your challenges, prepare yourself. Imagine the situation and envision being calm and collected. Acknowledge your triggers and remind yourself of your coping skills. Ask a friend for support, either before, during or after the event. Give yourself instant forgiveness if you're not as cool and able to cope as you'd hoped to be.

Many times, challenges come unexpectedly, heaping surprise on top of the already difficult issue. When you find yourself suddenly confronted by one of these challenges, remember:

- **Take your time.** Let your reactions cool and your response marinate. You don't have to answer or respond right away.
- **Make it impersonal.** Remind yourself, this discomfort is not about you and does not reflect upon the kind of person you are.
- **Look at the whole picture.** Consider the other participants. Try to see their vulnerabilities and their fears. Try to put things in perspective.
- **Look for the lessons and teachers.** Most of these "personal growth opportunities" strengthen us as communicators and as people. Notice what you are learning from this unlikely teacher.
- **Find the funny.** After the situation is over, look for the humor. See if you can turn it into a story to share with others.
- **Think about next time.** What did you do well? What would like to do better next time? Praise yourself and coach yourself.

Listening Abilities

Just as some feel the pen is mightier than the sword, so others believe the ear is mightier than the mouth. Earlier, we discussed Genuine Listening. Now, we're taking those FOCUS listening skills and going even deeper, seeking greater understanding and more meaningful communication. We're not only listening to the words, but we're practicing listening "between the lines" and "underneath the words" to what people are trying to express.

In this deep kind of listening, we want to distinguish between Facts and Truth. The Facts are the objective events—the who, what, where or when, uncolored by personality or emotional overlay. (As you might imagine, getting the facts is often challenging.) The Truth is the way the listener interpreted what happened—it's the world seen through their particular filter.

Finding the truth when the facts are fiction

When Miriam heard the upset client, she knew he had the facts wrong. She had to decide, "Should I remind him of the facts or should I try to discover his truth?"

Miriam chose to explore his truth by simply noticing and acknowledging his feelings and saying, "You sound upset."

With Miriam, this tactic worked smoothly. The man agreed; he was upset! Miriam was then able to concentrate on what the real issue was and how she could help him.

Acknowledging feelings takes practice and intuition. Here are some tips:

- Try to be general and empathetic. Instead of saying, "You sound angry," or "You sound irritated," which some people may take as criticism, try more neutral phrasing, such as:
  — "You sound upset."

  — "You sound uncomfortable."

  — "You sound as though you're dealing with a lot right now."

- Allow silence. When you mention someone's feelings, be prepared to have silent space, while they think or feel things through. Don't rush in with more words.

- Be flexible and be ready to hear a variety of responses when you make a comment about someone's emotions. Here are some different responses to the same statement:

- "You sound upset," you might say.
  — "No, I'm not upset. I'm just tired of people thinking everything is my fault!"
  — "I certainly am not upset with you. I just had a bad morning and I'm not over it."
  — "You'd be upset too, if people were always telling you that you sound upset."

Building relationships and trying for clear and honest communications is not easy. This kind of deep listening can be a test of your emotional reactions, attitude and responses. If people react strongly to your empathetic statements, try to read their body language and tone of voice. Are they frustrated, combative, confused or tired? Take a breath and sink into your intuition for your next response.

If they keep reacting to your words in a negative way, ask for help. You can simply say, "I apologize. I seem to be saying the wrong thing. Can you help me understand what you want to communicate?"

Emotional Releasing

Miriam was thrilled to be going to the recycling center. After her day at work, she needed a little emotional release. Yes, you can be green and "mean" at the same time. At Miriam's center, people were allowed to take their recyclable glass and throw it into the large metal bin. "Breaking glass makes such a satisfying sound," Miriam later told a friend.

This evening, Miriam had enough anger and irritation for dozens of jars or bottles. One for the gentleman who was so irritable on the phone. One for the computer company, which didn't provide the tech support as promised. One for that woman in the break room who glared at her. One for … Miriam left the recycling center feeling good and emotionally freer.

Almost every day, we deal with unfairness, incompetence, miscommunication, exhaustion and more. Naturally, our stress level soars. Creating time and space for emotional release prevents us from becoming angry or reactive communicators.

Make a quick list of ways you can factor in emotional release, both in and out of the office.

When you're office-bound

Ben wads up recycled paper and throws it against the wall when he's stressed. Miriam reorganizes her office. Joyce clears her mind by taking a moment to research a vacation on the Internet. Cassandra has colored pens and a doodle pad.

What are your office safety valves?

1. _____
2. _____
3. _____
4. _____

On lunch break

Brian goes to the gym every other day during lunch. Kate walks in the park to unwind from stress. Ellen lunches with a trusted friend once a week.

How can you feed your serenity during the lunch hour?

1. _____
2. _____
3. _____
4. _____

After hours

Of course, you know all about getting enough exercise, nutrition and rest. But emotional and stress release also calls for creating time for self-expression. That means pursuing a passion, doing something that lifts you up and restores your spirits.

What activities transport you, beyond stress, to your creative self?

1. _____
2. _____
3. _____
4. _____

Attitude

> *Everything can be taken from a man but ... the last of the human freedoms—to choose one's attitude in any given set of circumstances, to choose one's own way.*
>
> —Viktor Frankl, *Man's Search for Meaning*

The facts are going to remain the same, but you can change the "truth" by altering your attitude. For example, if a vendor is rude to you on the phone, you can either:

(a) Feel rotten the rest of the day—you can't believe the way that you were treated; or

(b) Figure he had a bad day and was just venting, and be glad you weren't rude in return

If you have to work late and are missing dinner with friends, you can believe that the boss is unjust and unfair and resent the extra work time. Or you can remember you were off early last week and look for the good that will come from the extra work.

If you are stuck in a long meeting, you can feel impatient and irritated at the way the boss is running the meeting or you can take some deep breaths and use the opportunity to make a list of to-do's.

Whenever it is appropriate, look at your attitude and at the way you are interpreting the facts. Here are a few questions to ask yourself:

- Am I making the situation personal when it isn't?
- Am I feeling negative emotions? Are these emotions helping me or harming me?
- Can I look at the situation more positively?
- Is there any action I can take?
- If there is no appropriate action, how can I use my attitude to help me move through the situation with ease and grace?

By lifting up your attitude and looking for the benefits, you increase your internal power and you have an easier and more pleasant time. Plus, you come across as a more agreeable and flexible person.

Responses to Others

"That's a lie. Jane is lying. I don't have to listen to this. I'm leaving."

Ellen looked around to see if anyone had picked up on her thoughts. Even though she had not spoken, the words blared through her mind. Thank goodness she had learned to think through her emotional reactions before she spoke.

But Jane hadn't. When the department manager changed a deadline, Jane went ballistic, saying she was the only one doing any work and no one else was pulling their weight!

"I'm grateful I can feel things," Samantha told Ellen after the meeting. "I'm also grateful I have enough inner strength, most of the time, to sift through my emotions and cool down before I speak."

We've all met people who spill out their emotions. Often these people gain a reputation for being volatile and unreliable.

It's healthy to feel emotions and it's even more constructive to use your inner powers to select which emotions you express in the workplace. When Jane reacted loudly, many people stopped listening to her. Some people are scared or uncomfortable during an emotional display. Often people don't trust those who pour out their feelings.

You want to be your authentic self in the workplace, and you want to effectively express your feelings in a calm, non-accusatory way. Learning how to communicate your emotions can add depth and credibility to your communications. Here are four tips:

1. **Learn to recognize when you are feeling emotional. Ask yourself:**
   - Where do I feel emotions in my body?
   - What kinds of situations trigger an emotional reaction?
   - What is my natural emotional reaction to a trigger?

2. **Take time to acknowledge your emotions and to understand them. Here are some questions to ask yourself:**
   - What am I feeling?
   - What thoughts or situations preceded this feeling?
   - How are these feelings related to past experiences in my life?

- What can I learn from these emotions?
- What, if any, action do I need to take? (This action can be as small as talking things through with a colleague. Or you may need to discuss your feelings with the person who triggered them.)

3. **If you do need to discuss your feelings, plan your conversation.**

   You may try the simple technique of stating the facts, stating your truth (your emotional response) and asking for what you want. For example, here's what happened between Sally and Kate:

   Three weeks after Kate felt snubbed by Sally, they were both at another meeting. Sally was delighted to see Kate and went up to talk to her. Kate, who was usually warm and welcoming, greeted her with a faint smile. Her eyes didn't light up and she didn't ask Sally how she was.

   Sally said, "Kate, you look pale. Are you not feeling well? Are you all right?"

   Kate took a deep breath. "I'm fine, Sally. But I feel confused and hurt by our last interaction."

   "What do you mean? We had a great talk last month."

   "Yes, but three weeks ago I went up you to at that agency meeting and you said 'Hello,' then you walked away without saying another word. I felt really hurt and confused. Can you help me understand what happened?"

   Sally knew exactly what Kate was talking about. She had been determined to speak to the President of the District and right after Kate came up, Sally noticed him. Instead of hurriedly explaining to Kate and excusing herself, she had simply rushed away.

   Once Sally apologized and explained, Kate felt better. She was glad that she had spoken up and not kept quiet about her hurt feelings. She was pleased to find out that Sally's behavior had nothing to do with her.

4. **Hope for results, and enjoy the process.**

   Communicating your feelings is an important component of developing your own inner power. Even if you don't get what you want, you still have the pleasure of clearly communicating your feelings.

The ELECTRIC Art of Building Inner Power

You don't want to be burning up with emotional righteousness and you don't want to be ice cold in your responses. You want to keep your cool and express your warmth. This chapter showed you how to further increase your communication skills by understanding and harnessing your inner power.

You've just explored ways to build these highlighted strengths:

- **Energy to pay attention and notice people**
- **Listening skills**
- Enthusiasm for people's answers and conversations
- Confidence that people want to talk to you
- Talking topics that draw people into the conversation
- Reaching-out abilities and a willingness to include everyone
- Interest in observing your surroundings and asking questions based on what you see
- **Connections that are meaningful**

Chapter 7:

Creating Champions:
Increase Your Visibility

Cassandra received an e-mail from her department manager.
"A gallery owner I know is looking for artists for a special showing. Tell him I sent you."

Cassandra was delighted to get this connection. She was trying to become more visible in the art community, so she could eventually move into a position in her company that required more fine arts skills. A gallery showing could be a pivotal step.

Her department manager had been receiving her e-letter, but months went by without him responding to the tips and information she sent. Two weeks ago, he had stuck his head in her office and said, "Thanks for keeping me on your e-mail list." Now he had sent information that could help her increase her visibility as an artist and also help her deepen her connections with the fine arts people.

Through her consistent, targeted communications, Cassandra was slowly building a network of business allies and widening her visibility.

The Champion in Your Corner

A champion or ally is someone who goes beyond pleasant or interesting conversation. A champion has many (or all, if you are lucky) of these characteristics:

- Knows who you are as a person and understands your goals
- Shows an active interest in you and your success
- Has a circle of influence that includes helpful connections or information
- Recognizes opportunities that are right for you
- Takes the time to communicate these opportunities
- Makes connections in your behalf and shares information that might be beneficial

Building Allies and Widening Influence

Cassandra spent a lot of time making connections and building relationships. She had many acquaintances and a number of friends. But most of her friends were not in positions to be helpful as business champions. She wanted to increase her champion base, so she began thinking beyond what she was already doing. She asked herself:

- **What am I doing to communicate and connect with people?**
- **What are people already doing for me?**
- **What more do I want?**
- **Which people or groups of people are potential champions?**
- **How can I become more connected to them and more visible?**

Here are Cassandra's answers:

- **What am I already doing to communicate and connect with people?**

  She sent out a monthly e-letter with tips for improving graphic design as well as tips for marketing art and writing. This e-letter went to about 100 people, including creative friends and colleagues and other people who asked to be put on the list.

  She invited people to lunch with her once every month or so. She sent this invitation to about 20 people who worked in her company and who she wanted to get to know better. Five or six came each time.

  She was watching for other ways to share meaningful information with people.

- **What are people already doing for me?**

  One friend kept Cassandra up on all the art showings in town. A colleague had invited her to be his guest at an arts fund raiser. Her company encouraged all employees to attend the Chamber of Commerce after-hours networking meetings. Occasionally someone sent her a graphic design article that was of interest.

- **What more do I want?**

  Cassandra wanted to expand her circle of friends and champions. She wanted to have at least seven people who were her champions, people who were connected within the graphic, artistic, business and philanthropic communities.

- **Which people or groups of people are potential champions?**

   The management team contained potential champions. People in complementary professions, such as writers and printers, were potential champions. Also people who were socially prominent or active in the volunteer community could be meaningful champions.

- **How can I become more connected to them and more visible?**

   Cassandra had some ideas but she wanted to broaden her own thinking. She decided to take this question and brainstorm with a few friends.

Five-step Communications for Champion-building

Answering Cassandra's questions will help you focus on cultivating your champions through communications.

As you write your answers, think of ways you enjoy connecting, sharing information or offering ideas. Your unique energy and sincerity will come through when you use communications pathways that feel natural and fun.

1. **What am I already doing?**
   Think of all the different ways you communicate with others. Think of individual e-mails you send, recommending a book or a restaurant. Think of conversations where you have an idea for someone. Make a thorough list.

2. **What are people already doing for me?**
   Who is helping you with career opportunities?
   Who wants you to be successful?
   Who sees your potential?

3. **What more do I want?**
   This is a key question. The more concretely you can define what you want, the more easily you can reach your goal.

4. **Which people or groups of people are potential champions?**

   Who can best help you meet your goals? Potential champions could include:

   - Friends or acquaintances you could build deeper relationships with; colleagues or managers who know of you and who have a circle of influence that could be helpful to you

   - Groups or associations of professionals in your field or in a complementary field

5. **How can I become more connected and visible?**

   Like Cassandra, you may want to set up a brainstorming session with friends. List your next steps. Make sure these are things you have the time and energy to do.

From Ideas to Influence

Cassandra came away from the brainstorming meeting with a page of communication ideas. She sorted them, grouping the similar suggestions and circling the ones that seemed most doable. She set aside ideas that were too time consuming, such as "Put on your own art show." "Become an art reviewer." "Try to get a column for the local arts magazine."

She chose the suggestions of expanding her e-letter readership because it made a lot of sense. "You're already doing the work," one of her friends said. "Why not share the information with more people?"

Cassandra agreed. She didn't have much spare time and she wanted to make the most of the work she put into the newsletter. Her expansion strategy included:

- Inviting her brainstorming friends to connect her with five people who would enjoy receiving the e-letter

- Asking the people already receiving the e-letter to forward it to five people who might enjoy it

- Asking her manager to identify other managers who might benefit from the graphics or marketing information

- Looking for newsletters that might appreciate an article offering graphic tips

- Asking her friends in complementary professions to suggest potential connections, either people who would enjoy the e-letter or organizations that might be interested in an article for their newsletter

Getting Their Attention Through Seven-R Communications

Once you've defined your goals, your potential champions and the resources you already have, you can use the Seven-R Theory of Champion Communications:

- **Really quick**—Accomplish a lot without spending much time
- **Relevant**—Offer information, thoughts or news that's meaningful to your audience
- **Regular**—Build the relationship with consistent communications
- **Reflect**—Show off your personality, talents and career goals
- **Reach wide**—Make the most of your time by reaching the most people
- **Remarkable**—Inspire people to stop and think. The more memorable the communication, the more likely people are to think of you again. Even one idea or phrase that's remarkable makes a difference.
- **Rare**—Reach out in ways that are unique

Rating Your Communications

Here's how Cassandra used the Seven Rs. Cassandra wanted to rate her e-letter expansion idea vs. the idea of selecting ten managers and sending them a personal card on special occasions. Here's her analysis.

- **Really quick**—Accomplish a lot without spending much time

  E-Letter: She could spend a modest amount of time and connect with hundreds of people.

  Personal Cards on Special Occasions: She could spend the same amount of time or more and connect with only a few people.

- **Relevant**—Offer information, thoughts or news that is meaningful to your audience

  E-Letter: Since each person on the mailing list had asked for the e-letter, the information was meaningful to the audience.

  Personal Cards on Special Occasions: She would be noticing information (a birthday or an award) instead of offering it, but her attention to those occasions would be meaningful.

- **Regular**—Build the relationship with consistent communications

  E-Letter: She could send out the e-letter consistently, monthly or bi-monthly.

  Personal Cards on Special Occasions: It might take months before the personal cards showed any kind of consistency. She couldn't overdo sending them, or it might seem like she was currying favor.

- **Reflect**—Show off your personality, talents and career goals

  E-Letter—She could easily reflect her personality, talents and career goals within the information and thoughts in the e-letter.

  Personal Cards on Special Occasions—She could reflect her personality in the notes she wrote.

- **Reach wide**—Make the most of your time by reaching the most people

  E-Letter: The newsletter could easily reach more and more people with little extra effort.

  Personal Cards on Special Occasions: These were targeted and limited communications.

- **Remarkable**—Inspire people to stop and think. The more memorable the communication, the more likely people are to think of you again. Even one idea or phrase that's remarkable makes a difference.

  E-Letter: She could add inspiring and targeted quotes for remarkable inspiration or do extra work and add her own ideas.

  Personal Cards on Special Occasions: She could add inspiring and targeted quotes for remarkable inspiration or do extra work and add her own ideas

- **Rare**—Reach out in ways that are unique

  E-letter: Sending out an e-letter was not unique. She would have to make sure its content was memorable.

  Personal Cards on Special Occasions: This was definitely a unique communication.

The ratings are just one tool for testing out your ideas. Intuition also plays an important role in building champions.

Intuition told Cassandra to expand the e-letter, paying more attention to it being reflective of her talents and career goals, as well as "remarkable." She would start a "rare" campaign with the managers she knew well, so her cards would seem natural and affirming rather than manipulative.

Increasing Your Power and Influence Through Visibility

"We have seen you everywhere," a colleague told Ben at lunch. "You were in the newspaper last week. And just the week before, I saw an article by you someplace else."

Ben smiled and thanked the man. He had actually written a column for a neighborhood newspaper, not the large circulation city paper. He also had a guest column in the local business journal the month before. But once you were published, most people just remembered you were in print and therefore assumed you were influential and knowledgeable. Even though Ben wasn't paid for either article, they were priceless in terms of increasing his influence.

Where can you be visible? Even writing a list of tips for a newsletter can increase your visibility. Volunteering and serving on a committee create extra visibility and interest. Make a quick list of options:

1. _____

2. _____

3. _____

4. _____

When Champions Mean Business

As a financial planner, Ben relied on referrals. That meant he had to create champions from customers, other professionals, friends and even vendors. He wanted to keep his champion base strong. Visibility was a key communications strategy for him.

Ben made himself visible by offering people information and entertainment. He budgeted a percentage of his earnings for champion-creation and client-building. He put on informational seminars, offering free lunches, usable information and networking opportunities for the attendees.

He also had a wide professional network that he regularly referred people to. He always followed through with both the person he referred and the professional, to see if the connection was made. This follow-through gave him the chance to reconnect with two important people, his professional colleague and his referee.

Building Champions Through Personalized Communications

"I can't imagine anyone wanting to receive any information from me," Ellen told Samantha, when Samantha shared the ideas about building champions. "I mean, all I do is think about marketing all day."

"You could capitalize on your marketing skills. But you're also very observant and you could capitalize on that," Samantha told her.

If you are observant and like to celebrate the details, you may be one of the "rare" breeds that can build champions through personal affirmations and attention.

"Rare" components include the ability to notice the remarkable events in people's lives and genuinely care about celebrating or affirming others.

These days, rare communications are the old-fashioned kind:

- Sending a greeting card complete with a hand-written note
- Making a congratulatory phone call
- Delivering an unexpected (but small) gift

You also can be unusual by:

- Remembering people's birthdays, when appropriate
- Donating to people's favorite causes or charities
- Showing up when people are doing special presentations

Select three people who are potential champions. Think of "rare" ways you can communicate with them. Try this for a year and notice the kinds of feedback you get.

Champion 1. Name: _____

Rare Communications: 1. _____

2. _____

3. _____

4. _____

5. _____

Champion 2. Name: _____

Rare Communications: 1. _____

2. _____

3. _____

4. _____

5. _____

Champion 3. Name: _____

Rare Communications: 1. _____

2. _____

3. _____

4. _____

5. _____

The ELECTRIC Art of Building Relationships

Experiment with your favorite ways to build champions and enhance your visibility. When you're true to yourself, this form of relationship creation will give you a lot of pleasure and a deep sense of purpose and connection.

In this chapter, we've discussed the following highlighted skills:

- **Energy to pay attention and notice people**
- **Listening skills**
- Enthusiasm for people's answers and conversations
- Confidence that people want to talk to you
- Talking topics that draw people into the conversation
- **Reaching-out abilities and a willingness to include everyone**
- **Interest in observing your surroundings and asking questions based on what you see**
- **Connections that are meaningful**

Chapter 8:

Playing Tough Roles:
Deliver Constructive Feedback

Joyce dreaded the upcoming conversation. Miriam had been a stellar employee for two years, but Joyce had recently received complaints from three different clients that Miriam had been "short" with them on the phone. Joyce prided herself on client communication; she couldn't afford to let another day or another client communication go by without discussing the issue with Miriam.

The Five Features of Fabulous Feedback

Before Joyce set up a meeting time, she reminded herself of the Five Features of Fabulous Feedback:

1. Forget any personal issues or triggers you may have around the subject

2. Find something to appreciate in the person's behavior

3. Focus on the facts. Discuss a specific incident

4. Follow through with questions

5. Forge a collaborative solution

1. Forget any personal issues or triggers

When Joyce had heard the client complaints, she felt furious. She was outraged that someone had not treated *her* clients properly.

"I don't usually get angry," Joyce told her co-worker Ben.

Ben reminded her of a story she had told him years ago. When Joyce had started her career as a financial planner at a large firm, she had not understood the importance of client cultivation. Her boss had chosen a team meeting to criticize Joyce's treatment of clients. Joyce felt her face flush when Ben mentioned the incident. She still remembered the embarrassment she had felt at that public criticism!

When Joyce moved into her current venture, she made sure that she and her team were totally client-centered. Now, along with concern for her business and her reputation, the old feelings of embarrassment and failure flooded into her.

Before she met with Miriam, Joyce tried to check her emotional state. Was her stomach clenched? Her throat tight? She decided if she felt any sudden rushes of emotion when she was talking to Miriam, she would take time out to calm herself.

To check your own objectivity on an issue, ask yourself these questions:

- What feelings come up when I think of this topic?
- What are those feelings related to? (You may not know the answer to this.)
- How do those feelings manifest?
- What will I do when I notice those emotions? (One example includes breathing deeply and letting go of negative thoughts.)

2. Find something to appreciate in the person's behavior

Miriam had been a wonderful employee for several years. In fact, Joyce did not remember the last time she had been displeased with Miriam. (She also realized she did not remember the last time she had praised Miriam.) Joyce wanted to appreciate behavior that was client-centered. She also wanted to be specific in her praise.

When she and Miriam were seated at the small table in her office, Joyce said, "I realized when I set up this meeting that it's been weeks since I've thanked you for all the work you do updating the client data base. I know you spent an extra hour just last Friday, organizing E-cards for the upcoming week. Your idea to keep track of birthdays, anniversaries and other special occasions has really built a lot of client loyalty."

The more specific the praise, the more meaningful. Joyce went beyond "great job of honoring clients," and mentioned details. This let Miriam know that Joyce was paying attention to her, acknowledging her innovations and noticing the extra work she put in.

Praise pays

Spreading positive feedback and appreciation is an effective way to acknowledge and encourage good work and to build relationships. Often, people are too busy to notice the good; many people only stop to fix something.

As you look around your workplace, watch for little excellences. Then take a moment to applaud that person. The more timely the appreciation and the more details you mention, the more powerful the praise is. This kind of honest communication takes minutes and gives people a long-lasting boost. Appreciation communication also helps you deepen your connections and helps people remember you.

Think of three colleagues whose work you admire. What kind of sincere praise could you give them? How could you effectively deliver the praise? Appreciating someone in person is most powerful, but often not practical. An e-mail, phone call or note will also work well.

1. Name: _____

   Praise: _____

   How and when: _____

2. Name: _____

   Praise: _____

   How and when: _____

3. Name: _____

   Praise: _____

   How and when: _____

Pay yourself with praise

Notice how you feel when someone praises your work. For most of us, this doesn't happen often enough. That's why it's important to notice and appreciate your own excellence and effort. When you've worked on a difficult project, give yourself a little praise. It's as simple as saying (or whispering), "Good job." Have fun with this concept. Grant yourself a gold star or a smiley face. Give yourself a pat on the back. These small gestures lift your spirits and add to your energy.

3. Focus on the facts

Joyce remembered an evaluation meeting with her old boss that was a fiasco. He spoke in vague terms and used no concrete examples. "You always," "You seldom," "Someone told me." He was dissatisfied, but had no specific requests for change. Joyce left the meeting feeling frustrated and confused. Was he venting his own unhappiness on her? Or did he really want her to change her behavior? If so, he had given her no specifics.

With Miriam, Joyce was careful to describe the incidents that concerned her.

"Mr. Tern called last week and wondered if you were OK. He said you had been impatient with him on the phone Tuesday and he said that was unusual. I wasn't too worried about that—I know how he can be. But Friday when I received phone calls from Mrs. Hander and Ms. Lee, with similar information, I became concerned. I didn't want to take any action until you and I had a chance to talk."

When describing the problem, the more open and honest you are, the more the person can understand the issue and respond appropriately. The goal is to describe specific actions and behaviors so the individual can change. Make notes if you're nervous providing the feedback or worried you might omit important information.

When you're delivering feedback and telling someone about a complaint regarding his or her behavior, try to include this information:

- Who complained?
- Who did they complain to?
- When did they complain?
- What did they say?
- What did they want to happen?
- What action have you already taken?

If you are receiving feedback, use the prior list to make sure you receive all the information you need to understand the content of the criticism or the complaint.

4. Follow through with questions

Though Miriam listened quietly, Joyce noticed her hands were clenched.

"I wanted you to have all the information I have," Joyce said. "Now, can you tell me what happened from your point of view?"

"I feel terrible," Miriam said. "Last week was overwhelming. I had to help Ben, since his assistant was ill. I felt torn between really giving my all to people or paying a little attention to everyone. I am so sorry that I upset these clients."

"Is the information they gave me accurate?"

"I don't feel I was rude," Miriam said. "But I was probably not as welcoming as I usually am."

"I'd love to hear your version of the conversations. Do you remember them?" Joyce asked.

Miriam remembered one of the conversations. Joyce agreed—Miriam had not been rude but she had not been her usual understanding self.

"What else should I know about this issue?" Joyce asked.

Miriam lowered her head. "I can't think of anything right now."

Joyce wanted to make sure she heard Miriam's side of the story. For some people and situations, you may need a series of questions to understand the true nature of the incident. Create a list in advance. End with an open question, such as "What else do you want me to know?"

5. Forge a collaborative solution

As she listened to Miriam, Joyce felt she was partially to blame for the situation. She had not noticed how burdened Miriam was. She had not hesitated to volunteer Miriam's services to Ben.

"Why didn't you tell me you were overwhelmed?" Joyce asked.

"I thought I could handle it all," Miriam said. "I didn't want to bother you."

"Next time, I want you to tell me right away. We'll work something out together. Meanwhile, how shall we solve the current problem and how can we prevent this from coming up again?" Joyce asked.

"I'll call the clients, if you wish, and apologize," Miriam offered.

"Are you comfortable doing that?"

"Yes. I can also send them a card, you know. I think they'll really appreciate that."

"Great. How does the rest of this week look for you? We can set some priorities together, so you don't feel so frustrated."

"I think I'm OK," Miriam said. "But maybe you should look at my to-do list and tell me what I can leave out, if I need to."

Joyce left the session feeling better. She felt the problem was solved. Preventing the situation from recurring was more challenging.

With Joyce and Miriam, client satisfaction was an agreed upon common ground. In situations that are more complex, you may have to work harder to establish your common ground. You are answering the question: What do you both want and how can you work together to get there? You may need additional brainstorming and problem solving to find a collaborative solution.

A Sixth F—Find Time to Give Ongoing Feedback

This issue gave Joyce some valuable feedback. She realized she needed to make time to give ongoing feedback to Miriam and her other staff. She needed to notice what they were doing right and she needed to train them on how to improve their customer service skills.

She decided to make it a point to add appreciations into her weekly Monday morning meeting with Miriam. She knew the importance of praise in the business setting, but like so many busy managers, she had not made this a priority.

Later that week, Ben sent her an e-mail: "After hearing about your issues with Miriam, I'm going to start giving my staff more positive feedback." He included a study of more than 500,000 employees in 300 companies (the Hay Group in 1999) that found "recognition for work well-done" was one of the 10 most important reasons people stay with a company.

Fashioning Feedback

Constructive feedback is collaboration, not criticism. You are using a problem to look for common solutions and to create a more efficient workplace. In this chapter, you have focused on constructive feedback tools that work well for almost any situation.

You've mastered the Five-plus features and you've used the highlighted ELECTRIC skills:

- **Energy to pay attention and notice people**
- **Listening skills**
- Enthusiasm for people's answers and conversations
- Confidence that people want to talk to you
- Talking topics that draw people into the conversation
- Reaching-out abilities and a willingness to include everyone
- Interest in observing your surroundings and asking questions based on what you see
- **Connections that are meaningful**

Chapter 9:

Going Beyond the Tabloids:
Handle Criticism, Wisecracks and Gossip

Ellen was furious at Jane. *Every time Ellen got the nerve to speak up in the brainstorming portion of the weekly team meeting, Jane muttered a derogatory comment.*

"Brilliant, Sherlock," Jane would say, rolling her eyes after Ellen spoke, or "I don't see how that could work" or "You don't seem to have a grasp of the big picture."

Ellen hoped her boss would notice Jane's negative jibes, but Jane was careful to keep her comments quiet and he didn't notice or didn't hear them. Ellen wanted to continue her quest to be a better communicator at work, but her confidence plummeted after every remark from Jane.

"She's criticizing me in front of everyone," Ellen told Samantha.

"Ignore her," Samantha advised.

Ellen tried, but she couldn't ignore her own hurt feelings. Samantha reminded her to tune into her inner power. After much tuning in and much thought, Ellen decided she wanted to say something to Jane.

"She may not acknowledge her behavior," Samantha warned Ellen.

"I don't care. I want to take action," Ellen told her.

In-your-face Issues: Criticism and Wisecracks

Stand firm and stand above criticism by using the STILTS approach in dealing with criticism and wisecracks:

- **S**ee beyond the emotions (yours and theirs)—listen for the actual content
- **T**ry to understand what motivates the criticism
- **I**ndicate you have heard them
- **L**earn more—ask them for more information
- **T**ell your side of the story
- **S**eek a solution

S - See beyond the emotions

Ellen remembered how she had been teased in high school. She was too old to be teased and she had worked too hard on boosting her own self-esteem to let Jane demoralize her.

During one meeting, Ellen wrote down each of Jane's wisecracks. Just the act of writing down Jane's jibes calmed Ellen: on paper, the remarks seemed sophomoric and harmless.

Think of people who often are sarcastic or critical towards you. The next time you're around them, try to separate your emotional reaction from what they are actually saying. You can do this by simply writing down some of their critical remarks. For example, Jane's notes might look like this:

- Situation: Weekly team meeting
- People who criticize me: Jane
- What she said: "That is a ridiculous idea. That will never work. "
- How I felt: Embarrassed, angry, criticized, picked on, isolated (Notice all the feelings those words brought up for Ellen. We all have our trigger areas and it's important to understand those.)
- What I want to do about it: During the meeting, I wanted to stand up and loudly defend myself
- What I intend to do about it: I really want to wait and analyze the best approach

Now make your own list.

- Situation: _____

- People who criticize me: _____

- What he/she said: _____

- How I felt: _____

- What I want to do about it:_____

- What I intend to do about it:_____

T - Try to understand what motivates the criticism

"Look at it like this," Samantha advised. "When someone is criticizing you, they're often mirroring things they don't like about themselves. Maybe Jane is insecure about the quality of her ideas. Maybe she's afraid to speak out in meetings. Instead of risking looking stupid, she goes on the offense and attacks you."

Ellen listened carefully to Samantha. When she thought of Jane as a vulnerable person who battled self-doubt and fear, she felt a little more compassionate. She also felt more powerful and less daunted.

What are the person's admirable qualities?

Ellen decided to list the things she admired about Jane. Even though it was a short list, she figured it would help her focus on the positive aspects of Jane. She wrote: "Gets things done on time; sees the potential in small ideas sometimes; says what she thinks."

Make a quick list of positive attributes of the person who criticizes you. Use this list when you begin the process of gathering information.

Qualities I admire in the person who criticizes:

1. _____

2. _____

3. _____

I - Indicate you have heard them

Ellen had been ignoring Jane's remarks. But now that Ellen understood a little more about the critical personality, she was ready to acknowledge and possibly confront Jane. At the next meeting, when Jane made a withering remark, Ellen took a deep breath and said, "I understand you feel my idea is lacking substance." She spoke calmly and looked at Jane in an open and friendly way. (At least she hoped her look came across as friendly. She was battling a mixture of emotions, some of them decidedly unfriendly!)

Jane seemed startled by Ellen's remark. She sat up straighter. "What do you mean?" she said tersely.

"You just said, 'What a stupid remark.' I take it that you think my idea is not well thought out."

"That's correct," Jane said.

For a moment, Ellen felt flustered. Then she took her next faltering steps on her STILTS.

L - Learn more

"What makes you uncomfortable with the idea?" Ellen asked earnestly. "What would make it better?" Her calmness seemed to unsettle Jane.

"The idea is not actionable," Jane finally answered. "You often speak without thinking."

"You're good at seeing the potential in things," Ellen said. This was one of the things she admired—Jane could often take a wisp of an idea and envision its potential benefits.

"What would it take to make the idea actionable?"

Ellen listened as Jane answered. Jane did have some good points. And since Ellen had asked for the information, she felt more like she was in a conversation than in combat.

Listening to the criticism

When you invite someone to give you additional information, you have a chance to learn more about that person and about yourself. Listen and ask yourself:

- Is there validity in what this person is saying?
- How can I benefit from the information?
- Does this person understand me and what I am saying?

Here are Ellen's answers:

- Is there validity in what this person is saying?

  Ellen thought that Jane did have some valid points.

- How can I benefit from the information?

  Ellen saw how much Jane liked being asked a question. From listening to Jane, Ellen learned she could probably disarm Jane and invite her into a conversation when Jane started making her remarks. Ellen would be more comfortable and confident if she could talk reasonably with Jane.

- Does this person understand me and what I am saying?

Ellen did not think Jane understood her at all. She felt Jane had judged her without truly listening. So she proceeded to tell Jane more.

T - Tell your side of the story

After Jane was finished talking, Ellen said, "Now I'd like to take a minute and tell you why I offer such ideas and comments."

Ellen succinctly described her own thinking process.

"Since we're brainstorming, I like to throw out ideas, intending them to be catalysts for others to improve on," she said. "The more freely we can each express ourselves, the greater the possibility one of us will come up with an actionable idea."

Ellen was proud of herself for staying focused and not mentioning how Jane's comments made her feel.

S - Seek a solution

"You each bring up good points," her boss finally spoke. "What's the best way to handle this issue?"

"I'd like to be able to share ideas and if Jane believes an idea needs help, she could acknowledge that by simply saying something like, 'Interesting idea. It would be even stronger if ....'"

Her boss looked at Jane, who shrugged.

"I can try," she said.

"Let's all try to do that," the boss said.

Ellen felt elated as she left the meeting. She had spoken out. She had suggested a solution. Now even if Jane went back to sniping, Ellen could more easily stop the harassment by reminding everyone of this supportive solution.

Look at yourself

As Ellen reflected on how Jane's negative remarks made her feel, she wondered if she ever made such careless comments to people. She vowed to watch her own remarks more carefully and to more fully acknowledge and affirm other people's ideas.

Behind Your Back: Defuse Gossip

Carol was in the center of a small group of people in the break room. When Samantha walked in, Carol stopped talking. Samantha wondered what was going on. Was Carol talking about her? Lately Samantha had heard about e-mails Carol was sending out, spreading rumors about George and a few other people. Samantha wondered what Carol was up to.

She soon found out when Ellen called and said, "I heard you got into trouble over the Horton project. Are you all right?"

"I'm fine. And I'm not in trouble. I just had to redo a section of the proposal. It's normal procedure. Who told you I got into trouble?"

"Carol," Ellen said. "I should have known better than to believe her."

Samantha didn't want to be in the middle of a gossip storm. She decided to use the STILTS approach to deal with Carol:

- S - See beyond the emotions (yours and theirs)—listen for the actual content

  Samantha was irritated but not made overly emotional by Carol's gossip. She knew what Carol was saying about her was not true.

- T - Try to understand what motivates the gossip

  Samantha knew Carol was needy. Carol's need to be accepted and important was probably turning her into a gossip, possibly a dangerous gossip.

- I - Indicate you have heard them

  Samantha decided to talk to Carol. She dropped by Carol's office to see if she had a moment. Then she told Carol, "I wanted to check with you on something I heard. Were you telling people I was in trouble over the Horton project?"

- L - Learn more—ask them for more information

  "Did you say that?" Samantha asked.

  "That's what I heard," Carol said.

  "From whom?" Samantha asked.

  "Well, I overheard you had to redo the proposal," Carol confessed.

- T - Tell your side of the story

  "I appreciate your concern, but redoing sections of a proposal is quite normal," Samantha said. "Maybe you don't understand the steps of creating a proposal. Would you like me to explain, so next time you'll understand?"

  Carol nodded sheepishly.

  Samantha outlined the proposal process, then asked if Carol had any questions.

- S - Seek a solution

  "The next time you hear something about me, please feel free to come right to me and find out if it's true," Samantha suggested when the conversation ended.

  Carol agreed.

  Samantha didn't know if Carol would follow through on their informal agreement. She decided to invite Carol to participate in a volunteer project Samantha was coordinating. Perhaps that would help her feel needed in a more constructive way.

Searching the mirror

Like Ellen, Samantha used her experience with Carol to take a look at herself. She liked analyzing and thinking about other people. Was she guilty of spreading gossip? She vowed to be more careful about how she talked about people in the workplace.

Being Wise—and Wisecracks, Criticism and Gossip

It's tempting to talk about the various personalities at work, but too many careless words to the wrong kind of person can ruin a person's reputation and can poison the atmosphere at work.

In this chapter, you used your ELECTRIC power to handle criticism and enhanced your:

- Energy to pay attention and notice people
- Listening skills
- **Enthusiasm for people's answers and conversations**
- Confidence that people want to talk to you
- Talking topics that draw people into the conversation
- **Reaching-out abilities and a willingness to include everyone**
- **Interest in observing your surroundings and asking questions based on what you see**
- **Connections that are meaningful**

Chapter 10:

Lighting Up Your Conversation:

Speak Persuasively
and to the Point

Being a persuasive speaker takes more than confidence *and articulation. You need to deliver information, potential benefits and a specific request in an enthusiastic and accessible way. As you build your persuasive powers, you'll also be increasing your influence, your champion base and your career.*

Ellen could feel the tension in the room as Carl took the floor. The marketing team had worked on this presentation for weeks—getting to know the vendor and his needs, crafting the proposal, creating the PowerPoint® presentation, and writing a dynamic script. But last week, Carl, the group manager, had suddenly decided he wanted to give the key presentation. And what's more, he did not want to use the script they had so carefully prepared.

"I know these people," he had told them. "I'll look at the script and deliver the information my way."

Several of the team were relieved Carl was giving the presentation. That way, if something went wrong, none of them would take the blame. Others felt uncomfortable—Carl was a good speaker, but he could get off topic and they only had 30 minutes.

Ellen admired the easy way Carl addressed the group, as if they were friends in his living room. She also admired the short joke he started with. But he was 20 minutes into his talk and had not delivered the key components of the proposal. She looked around. Several people from the vendor's team were doodling or text messaging. She hoped Carl would hurry and get into the substance of the presentation.

A+ Persuasion Powers

To enhance your A+ Persuasion Powers, try these simple techniques:

- Analyze your audience. Understand their needs and how they think.
- Articulate a clear message in a concise manner. Don't make people guess at what you want.
- Add up the benefits: Let the audience know—What's in it for them? the company? you? others?
- Allow your enthusiasm to show. Your honest enthusiasm can inspire and motivate people.
- Answer questions and concerns. Involve and include the audience by inviting comments and suggestions.
- Ask for what you want, but don't push.

Here are some ways to put these persuasive pointers to use.

Analyze your audience. Understand their needs and how they think.

Brian had promised to deliver a project by mid-month. But as he delved into the project, he realized that both he and his boss had omitted a key component. Including that component could mean delaying completion by an additional two weeks, but it would take the finished product from good to outstanding. Brian knew he could do outstanding work, but often his strategic and creative thinking skills were not challenged on the job. He wanted to persuade his boss to give him the extra time and latitude on the project.

Brian knew his boss well. His boss prided himself on running a department that never missed a deadline. Reliability and bottom line were important. Brian would need a compelling reason for changing the timeline.

To analyze your audience, think of someone you want to persuade. Ask yourself these questions:

- What values are important to them?
- What principles do they feel strongly about?
- What kinds of issues motivate and inspire them?
- When have you seen them change their minds about something important?

Articulate a clear message in a concise manner

Sharon was talking, but what was she actually talking about? Brian could tell by Sharon's earnest expression that she had something important she wanted to say. He wished she would hurry up and say it.

When you're trying to persuade someone, be a headliner. Imagine the front page of a newspaper. Headlines rule. Before you read an article, headlines draw you in and give you the scoop.

Brian knew he had to be a headliner to keep his boss's attention. Before creating his talking points, he asked himself:

- What facts does my boss need to know?
- What extra information will make him more comfortable?
- What is the most important point?
- What end result do I want?

Keep these points in mind as you gather information, analyze the benefits and create your opening.

Add up the benefits: Let the audience know—What's in it for them? the company? you? others?

Brian researched the potential benefits of broadening the project scope. The benefits to his boss included: higher visibility in the industry, increased client satisfaction, a product component they could incorporate into other projects and the potential for revenue increase.

The downside for his boss was changing a deadline. While he would not be spending more money, his boss would be losing Brian's time. Brian believed that increased orders from this client and the potential to market the idea would minimize the cost.

Brian listed the benefits to his boss, the company and himself. Brian's benefits included: a chance to display his talents, a chance to be innovative, a chance to be more visible in his field and potentially have more work flowing into his department.

Brian believed the project was beneficial for him, his boss and the company.

A+ EXTRA:

Admit when you are benefiting. Be honest about your own potential benefits. Ideally, your company wants you to be satisfied at work.

Allow your enthusiasm to show. Your honest enthusiasm can inspire and motivate people.

That evening, Brian shared his enthusiasm about this project with his wife. She was fascinated. Brian wanted to feel the same level of enthusiasm when he presented the information to his boss the next day.

At the meeting with his boss, Brian spoke in a firm and expressive voice. He used dynamic gestures but was careful not to get too carried away. His boss did not appreciate drama. He allowed his enthusiasm to build as he added up the benefits. He could see his boss leaning forward, and that helped Brian maintain his high level of energy.

Answer questions and concerns. Involve and include your audience by inviting comments and suggestions.

Invite questions and feedback. The more questions people ask, the more you can help them understand the scope of what you are saying. This understanding can potentially increase their involvement and support.

You can also ask questions, to make sure the audience understands your message.

The more people discuss their questions and concerns with you, the more information and ideas you can offer to help alleviate any issues or resistance. Don't be afraid of silence. Give people time to think through what you've said and to formulate questions and feedback.

Ask for what you want, but don't push

"I'd like for us to approach the client with this new information and see if we can agree on a new deadline," Brian said, at the end of his presentation.

Brian asked for what he wanted and slightly more. He did want to be part of the presentation to the client, but if his boss preferred to go solo, Brian didn't mind.

He knew his boss did not like to make quick decisions. Brian ended by saying, "I know you'll want to think this over. Let me know if you need any more information."

Who persuades you?

To further hone your persuasive style, think about who influences you. The more you recognize the qualities of a persuasive conversation, the more effective you'll be at explaining your points.

Here are two examples:

- When Samantha heard Barbara was coming by for lunch, she tucked her wallet into her pocket. Barbara was always involved in some fascinating volunteer project and Samantha knew she would want to make a small donation. Barbara had a gift for quickly explaining the need and the facts and then sharing her passion about the project and its benefits. Samantha didn't have much time to volunteer, but she loved being swept up by Barbara's enthusiasm.

- Ben was booked up with speaking engagements, but when Alan asked him to speak to a business networking group, he found himself saying yes. Alan had a direct communication style that Ben appreciated. Alan came right out with his request, listing the reasons that Ben was the ideal speaker for his group. He told Ben the number of people, their range of professions and the possible benefits for Ben. Alan's command of the facts, the benefits and his knowledge of both Ben and the audience persuaded Ben to accept the engagement.

Activating Personal Persuasion Power

Think about the people you like to say "yes" to. Make a quick list of their persuasive qualities. Consider Samantha's and Ben's examples: What role do information, enthusiasm, direct communication, etc., play for you?

1. _____

2. _____

3. _____

4. _____

5. _____

What Is Your Persuasion Program?

Ellen wondered why she wasn't more persuasive. After brainstorming with Samantha, she made a list of her strengths and challenges in persuading people. Here's what she came up with:

Ellen's strengths:

- Good listener
- Good at checking for understanding
- Good at paying attention to what people say
- Able to plan and organize talks, laying out the benefits and facts

Ellen's challenges:

- Tamps down her passion; does not speak enthusiastically
- Does not speak directly; takes too long to get to the point when it's important
- Doesn't follow through and ask for what she wants

Think about your own gifts and challenges. Make your own list.

My strengths:

1. _____

2. _____

3. _____

4. _____

My challenges:

1. _____

2. _____

3. _____

4. _____

The Art of Persuasion Practice

Ellen decided to practice on Kate. She shared her list of challenges and put together a short speech persuading Kate to eat lunch with Ellen at a certain restaurant.

Then she practiced over the phone with Kate, who helped Ellen amp up her enthusiasm and coached her to make her request more direct. Ellen made three phone calls before Kate approved of her persuasion skills and felt genuinely excited about eating at the restaurant.

Ellen then began working on how she would persuade her manager to pay for her membership in the marketing association. Samantha agreed to coach her on this project.

Everyday persuasions

You can start persuasion practice with co-workers and friends. Begin with little things and notice what kinds of response you get. Notice where you shine and where you thud. Ask for feedback. Then move into the workplace and use the art of persuasion to move your career forward.

ELECTRIC Persuasion Power

In this chapter, you learned about A+ Persuasion Powers. You learned how to put together information and benefits, how to generate feedback and ask for results. As you become increasingly persuasive, you will continue to enhance these skills, using your ELECTRIC template. You'll be using:

- **Energy to pay attention and notice people**
- **Listening skills**
- **Enthusiasm for people's answers and conversations**
- **Confidence that people want to talk to you**
- Talking topics that draw people into the conversation
- **Reaching-out abilities and a willingness to include everyone**
- Interest in observing your surroundings and asking questions based on what you see
- **Connections that are meaningful**

With your own natural gifts and talents and the tips you've found in this book, you now have everything you need to be an ELECTRIC communicator.